HELP!
MY COMPANY
SWIPED LEFT!

Jill L. Ferguson
&
Laura C. Browne

In Your Face Ink LLC

© 2023 In Your Face Ink LLC and Jill L. Ferguson and Laura C. Browne
All rights reserved, including the right to reproduce this book or portions thereof in any form whatsoever.
Interior Design and Cover Design by Rick Schank, Purple Couch Creative
Manufactured in the United States
Library of Congress Cataloging-in-Publication Data has been applied for.
ISBN: 978-0-9765659-5-6 (hardback)
ISBN: 978-0-9765659-7-0 (paperback)
ISBN: 978-0-9765659-8-7 (ebook)

Table of Contents

CHAPTER 1
My Company Dumped Me...Now What?...................................... 4

CHAPTER 2
How To Recover From the Breakup 14

CHAPTER 3
Don't Go Into Armadillo Mode 29

CHAPTER 4
Come Out of Your Shell and Turning Leaving
Into Learning 39

CHAPTER 5
How To Get Back Out There 51

CHAPTER 6
Interviews: How to Shine Bright Like a Diamond 57

CHAPTER 7
How to Know When You Should Swipe Right 71

CHAPTER 8
Create the Work Relationship of Your Dreams 81

CHAPTER 9
You Can Do It! 88

Thank you 92

The Authors 94

CHAPTER 1

My Company Dumped Me... Now What?

WELCOME TO THIS BOOK. If the title made you laugh or cringe or coil in fear, you may be in the right place. We live in a time when companies, like people, aren't very loyal. They expect a lot from those who receive their direct deposited paychecks, and at the first sign of trouble, they may look for people and places to cut. Just as some people flee relationships at the first bit of rockiness, companies may dump individual contributors, whole departments or divisions, and/or the bottom percentage of its salesforce at any given time.

And when your company breaks up with you, it hurts. It hurts a lot. And you may wonder, was it me? Or was it them?

We're here to help you navigate through the unknown and the difficult times. And why, you may wonder. Well, we've been there. Laura has spent many years in corporate human resources and was let go unexpectedly twice, including one time when she was laid off by a manager who left her a brief voicemail saying her job was eliminated and that was her last day. This was only slightly better than being broken up with over text or social media. But it still stung. Rejection of any kind is painful. And somehow when the person dumping you lacks the *cojones* to tell you to your face, the rejection feels worse. It's like you aren't important enough for them to make the time.

Jill's experience came in her 20s, during a high level job that ended when it was discovered that the past executive stole and laundered money through the organization and created such a complicated mess that the nonprofit was forced to close its doors forever. The ex-exec was sent to federal prison in Texas, while the people she left behind at the company were out of their jobs.

Regardless of how it happens to you or under what circumstances, suddenly losing your job sucks. It makes you question life, what you could have done differently, your value as a worker and a person of knowledge and action, and sometimes even your worth.

Having your company swipe left can invoke a serious pity party. But before we break out too many Kleenex, pints of ice cream, or drink too much wine or hard seltzer, let's figure out a way to make the best of a shitty situation.

Take a deep, cleansing breath. Repeat: it's those mo-fos and not me. It's those mo-fos and not me. It's those mo-fos and not me. And read on.

OMG I'm in Shock

What happened to you? Did you get called in to your manager's office expecting a routine meeting only to find out that your job was being eliminated? Or worse, did your boss ask to talk to you and you thought you were finally getting that bonus or raise for the kick-ass job you've been doing, only to find HR in the room, raining on your party and saying you were being let go? Or maybe you were summoned to an all-hands meeting and everyone in the room and/or on the video screen was told at the same time that your jobs were gone? That's one time where a room full of people feels lonely AF.

Whatever way you got the news, it seriously sucks. You may feel like your insides have been ripped out. You may find it difficult to breathe. And you may question yourself. You may wonder how you are going to pay for that new car or house or big ticket item you just bought. And you may be panicked about how quickly you can find another job. We get it. Especially when Bankrate and other media report that forty percent of Americans don't have enough in savings to cover a large unexpected expense of $1000 or more. If that's you, your chest may be feeling tight and your head may be spinning. But don't let despair set in.

Take a deep breath. Hold that air in like oxygen is your

lifeline, because, well, it is. And then blow it out through your mouth with all of your might. Flare those nostrils and breathe in deeply. Expand your chest and fill it with air. Hold it for the count of five, and then swoosh that stale air out. And do it again if you have to until you feel your sadness and anger subside a bit.

And now let's deal with the shock.

When you got the bad news, your head may have started spinning and the rest of the meeting may have been a blur. You may feel like you've sunken like the Titanic. And maybe you can't imagine that it will get better. But it will. Trust us on this.

We get why you may be in shock. Even if you knew that companies were tightening up and maybe letting people go, you probably thought that was other companies and other people, not you. You'd been doing a good job and thought the company was doing well. Or even if you thought your company was struggling, you certainly didn't think it would affect you like this. So shock (and sadness and anger and rage) are to be expected.

Acknowledge your feelings. Say hey, sadness, I feel you. Anger, of course you're erupting. Shit, I never saw this coming and I don't know what to do. Oh yeah, hopelessness, I feel you. I feel all of you chaotic emotions pummeling me from inside. Thank you, emotions, for trying to help and keep me safe. I appreciate that. But I know we can't be besties. Otherwise, you'll take me to a dark place.

Let us and this book be the flashlights that illuminate your darkness and guide you to sunshine or at least to a smidgeon of hope. :)

It's Not You, It's Them

Welcome to the current world of work where companies demand loyalty from you and say they love you until they don't. They say nonsense like we're all family until they sit you down with HR and tell you it's all about the numbers and the bottom line. And even though you think your salary is a drop in the bucket, HR is telling you that's one drop too many and you need to go.

Because your company probably professes to value their employees, you had good reasons to believe that you would continue to be employed and wouldn't be surprised like this. But the reality is you're not family. You're a worker in a job, and when that company doesn't see the immediate value of that job, you're done.

You might be part of a corporate layoff when the company is struggling with profits. You may have been doing an AMAZING job. You may have been beating all your quotas, BUT when the company looked at the numbers, your division or job didn't add up to exactly what they wanted.

Or you might be the only one let go either due to the fact that your boss doesn't see your value, doesn't like you, or wants to put someone else in your place. That sounds harsh, but bosses are people and are sometimes led by their moods and personal connections, and also they do whatever they need to make themselves look good.

Whether it's a corporate layoff or just one person who loses their job, it comes down to the same thing. You don't have a job and it's scary.

The reality is losing your job may have nothing to do

with you or your performance, unless your manager has put you on a performance plan or given you a written warning or a final warning. Otherwise, you were just in the wrong place at the wrong time.

And even if they did tell you that there was something lacking in your performance, you need to understand that might not be the full story. Some companies rank employees in every department yearly and insist that a specific number be the combined average. One major corporation (who will remain nameless so we don't get sued) uses the number 1. So if an employee is ranked a 1.4 that means someone else in their department must be a negative number in order to average 1 overall. It's a numbers game that barely reflects employee worth. But it is an example of how there are many times that managers want a certain result and so they must adjust the story to fit that result. It may not seem fair, but it happens...and all too frequently.

For another example, you might be doing a great job, but because another part of the company is not doing well, all departments have been told to cut 10 percent from the budget. Your manager is told that they must reduce headcount or salary expenditures by a certain number, and they are certainly not going to suggest that they lose their job or cut their salary. They're going to protect the jobs that make them look good and they'll protect their favorite employees. So they look at the other employees. They can take one piece of information, where there was a very minor issue, and turn it into a reason for you to be on the chopping block.

Is that fair? Of course not, but work isn't fair. Work is all about the numbers and the numbers may have nothing to do with you.

It doesn't matter how many weekends you've skipped your social life to be at the office or how many awards you won in the past or how many of your fellow team members or customers have thanked you for your work. When the company is looking to cut money from budgets, they forget all that.

And chances are that when you got the news from your boss or HR, you had one of three responses:

1. I screwed up! If only I had done more of (fill in the blank) or less of (fill in the blank) this would not be happening to me.

2. Those bastards, they suck. I hate them.

3. Woohoo! I hated this f-ing place anyway, and now I can get out, get some unemployment (and maybe some severance), and get something less soul-sucking.

If you relate to number one, you're like many people. We immediately beat ourselves up and wish we had done something differently.

STOP. It's not going to help you.

Yes, later when you're feeling better you can look at your experiences in the company to see what learnings you can use for the future. But now, when you're in shock, it's the time to be nice to yourself and cut yourself some slack. Eat some chocolate. Pour yourself a drink. Walk in the woods. Devour some nachos. Play a video game marathon. Run. Do whatever makes you feel better.

If you relate more to response two and you think they're all bastards, that can actually help you to get through this easier because you won't waste a lot of time blaming yourself. As long as you don't ruminate on why they were so bad or on being angry and vomit hatred for too many days, this attitude can help you move forward.

And if you are shocked but relieved by your sudden unemployed state, you're on the right track. Whether you hated your job or not, it obviously was not the right place for you. You now have an opportunity to start something new that can be much better, more rewarding, and better aligned with your values and desires.

What Not To Do

Take a deep breath and pause. We mean it. DON'T DO ANYTHING. This is your opportunity to go from a chronic human doing to a human being. Right after you are pushed from a job is not the time for quick or rash decisions. You need time to process and time to be kind to yourself.

If the company wants you to sign something (and they often do when they are pushing you out the door), you should:

- Breathe and be patient until your heart stops beating staccato in your chest.

- Stay professional.

- Say you will need time to think about this and will get back to them with questions. Don't be forced into quick decisions when you're in shock. Ask how long you have.

Do not:
- Sign anything until you have enough time to review it and really understand it.

- Say anything that you might regret. Silence is golden is a saying for a reason. And in the case of staying silent instead of spewing hatred during your corporate exit, it may be platinum and be the difference between people remembering you fondly or not.

- Try to get back at them by sending a final nasty email to others or by doing anything else that might be considered retaliatory (like a one-star review and trash talk on Glassdoor). It might feel satisfying at the time but could cause real problems for you, including legal problems.

The most important thing you can do is to take care of yourself and take the time necessary to make good decisions. Often companies will give you paperwork that you will need to sign in order to get severance or other things like outplacement services if you were part of layoff. If you're unsure how to deal with this, ask for help. Depending on the situation, you may want to talk with a lawyer before you sign anything to make sure you're making the best decision possible. Especially if what you are being asked to sign is an agreement not to sue the company.

If you're offered outplacement services, make sure you get the most out of them. If you need a week or two to clear your head, ask if you can delay the start of the services because you normally only have the outplacement for a certain amount of time.

And then, when you've done the paperwork and said goodbye, please, please, please, don't jump into the first job that you see or that makes you any kind of offer. (We will talk more about this in a future chapter.)

CHAPTER 2

How To Recover From the Breakup

"DATE YOUR JOB, DON'T MARRY IT" is the advice from a dear friend of Laura. There's a good reason for this. Once you've married your job, it's going to feel like you're going through a divorce, not just a breakup.

Let's look at how tough this divorce could be for you. How much do you identify with your job? If you really were able to casually date it and not get too attached, then this process will be a whole lot easier.

On a scale of 1–5, where a 1 means no, not much and a

5 means yes, very much, how would you rate the following questions?

___Were you employed by the company for a long time?

___Is your identity strongly connected with your old job? (If you've seen *Top Gun Maverick*, think of when Maverick says being a pilot is not what he is but who he is. Is this how you identify with your role?)

___Do you see your colleagues as good friends or family?

___Are unsure about what to do next?

___Do you feel that the change in employment will strongly affect your life?

If you have a score of 5-10, you probably weren't that connected to the job, which could help you move on more quickly and easily.

A score of 11-17 means that you could struggle some.

A score of 18-25 could mean that it's going to take time and effort to untangle your life from your old job or who you think you are/were.

Just like a breakup, you're going to move through different stages as you deal with this. A helpful way to view this is with Elisabeth Kubler-Ross' 5 Stages of Grief. You might be familiar with these stages as they connect to death. But in this case we aren't talking about the death of a person, we are talking about the death of an identity: you as JOB TITLE @ X COMPANY. Of course, you're not dying but it can feel like that some days.

The first stage you've got to deal with is Denial. And that denial could have come before they even swiped left on you. After all, everything was going along fine, and you thought nothing was going to change. Maybe before you were told the news you heard rumors that the company might cut people. But you ignored it. Even if you saw negative news about your company or your company executives announced budget cutting measures, you may have convinced yourself that those are all good things that would PREVENT layoffs. It can be easy for us to convince ourselves that there's nothing to worry about if we don't want to see it.

Even after you heard about other people being affected and the HR person joined you in your meeting, you might still not have believed there was a problem.

But then they told you. You had to leave. And even as you packed up your stuff and handed back the company's property to security or IT or your manager, you still may not have believed the situation was real. But then it sinks in and you feel the weight of the rejection.

And the second stage, Anger, plows into you with the force of a bullet train. It's NOT FAIR you want to shout. For some people the anger starts as soon as they get the news. For other people, the anger is delayed until the shock wears off. The anger may be directed at yourself, at the person who gave you the message, at the company, or at the world in general.

As we already said, be kind to yourself. Getting pissed at yourself won't help. It also won't help for you to throw shade or lash out at your family and friends when they try to help you. They love you and are human like you and doing the best they can.

Then comes Bargaining, the third stage of grief (though let's be honest: You may have started this stage in the meeting with your boss and HR, when you found out the news). This is when you say that you'll do something differently or change if you can keep your job. This can be the part where you try to convince your boss to give you another chance so you don't have to look elsewhere. But it doesn't work. The decision has already been made.

Some people in this stage, in a fit of desperation with no moving forward job plan, apply to every job they see, even ones for which they are overqualified or underqualified. They just want someone, anyone, to want them. And if you've ever been around someone overly needy, you understand the unhelpful, almost repulsive, energy that neediness emits.

When that doesn't work, the next stage is Depression. This is different from clinical depression. This refers to a low point when you question your skills and worth and feel lacking and really awful. This depression could be a weekend where you can't get out of bed and gorge yourself on a steady diet of Lay's, Doritos, Cheetos, and Oreos, or a time when you go out and get really shit-faced drunk to forget the pain.

As you move through the tough times, you're on your way to Acceptance. It doesn't mean that you like what happened, but you adopt the attitude that shit happens and it happened to you, but you choose to move on.

We've provided this summary of the work of Elisabeth Kubler-Ross and talked you through the stages so you can recognize them and determine where you are. But it's important to acknowledge that working through these stages may not be super straightforward. Think about your love life. You may get to the point you feel great about a break-up. *Sayonara, dude. I don't need you any more.* But then what happens? You see a social media post of your ex having a great time with someone who isn't you and your anger may explode like a molotov cocktail. *Yo, bitch, that's my man.* And just like that, you emotionally regress. Except for work, that reaction may be triggered by a LinkedIn announcement of a colleague's promotion, someone's new job, or even a high school classmate's announcement of her new venture. It's natural to go back and forth emotionally when you've been hurt, but keep pushing ahead.

It's important that you give yourself time and space to go through the steps. For example, don't just smooth over the anger and say, "It's okay; everything is going to work out." Jump into it. Examine how you're feeling and roll in the mud. The goal is to get through to the other side of it and the way to do it is to wade in and experience it so you can deal with it.

What are you really angry about? Do you think your ex-manager is a horrible ass-kissing moron who cared more about sucking up than helping their employees? Good. Own it. Scream about it. Get it out.

Who or what makes you pissed off? Is it others? Your boss? Your company? Capitalism? The world?

Or are you mad at yourself? Sometimes until we really delve into our emotions we don't understand what is triggering us.

For example, Jill's friend, Dani, moved three-quarters of the way across the country for a job at a start-up. She realized a few months in that things weren't as she was told and the founder was stuck in doing things his own way, to the detriment of the company. After trying to be the change in the company to help it move forward, Jill's friend knew she and the founder must part ways.

Dani said, "I grew so frustrated and angry that I moved there and was misled. One day I couldn't take it anymore so I got in my car and went for a two-hour drive and I ranted to myself and screamed in the privacy of my vehicle. And then it hit me. I thought I was angry with the founder, the company, and the stupidity, but I was really angry at myself for my lack of discernment and taking the job and moving in the first place. I realized it was the same pattern I did in my romantic relationships."

When Dani understood that, she forgave herself and promised to honor her wants and needs and own intelligence above all else. That's when she let go of all of the anger and healed.

Until you can actually see what the deep-rooted feelings are and their causes, you can't heal from them and move to the next stage. Yes, it's really uncomfortable trying to move through Anger, Bargaining, and Depression, but it's necessary.

Other emotions you may experience after being dumped by your company include anxiety, distrust, fear, and shattered self-confidence. Let's talk about these one by one. Anxiety has been defined as feeling nervous, restless, or tense and these things may affect your heart rate, your breathing, may cause you to sweat, or feel trembly or weak. Anxiety can be triggered when you think about the bills you have to pay, if you're worried what your past co-workers think of you, at the dread of having to redo your resume and send out applications and face rejection. Anxiety can be caused by all kinds of things, big and small.

A close cousin of anxiety—which can make you worried and fearful—is distrust. You may suddenly not trust yourself or your own judgment (as in *How could I not have seen this coming? Clearly, I'm not good enough or smart enough or x enough.*) Or you may not trust companies in general, HR representatives or managers specifically, and/or decide all corporations are evil as they clearly don't care about anyone.

Throupled with anxiety and despair may be fear. You may be afraid you'll never find a good job or that if you do find one that you'll be dumped again. You may also fear how to answer questions at an interview regarding your past employment. Or you may fear what may be said when a potential employer calls your references or calls to confirm your employment with your past employer. And of course, there's the fear that you'll never feel safe working for someone again.

And that's because being let-go from your job can shatter your self-confidence.

Then there's the feeling of shame. Laura remembers a time when she was working as a contractor and her contract was unexpectedly changed from full-time to very part-time. One of the big problems was the shitty way that the message was delivered. When Laura protested that she wished she had known sooner because she had given up other contracts to focus on this one, the manager gave her a look of pity and said something to the effect of, "You poor thing, you should have known that this was going to end." Ouch! That was a real slap in the face. Laura left the meeting and went out to her car to cry. Laura ended up leaving that contract position as soon as she could.

Even if your manager and HR person don't say anything specific that could shame you, you may still feel embarrassed and devastated.

Move Forward

So how does one move forward? Here's a 3-step process to help you to navigate through this difficult time. The steps are rather simple but are quite effective. They are:

Step 1: Question it
Step 2: Say it
Step 3: Rewrite it

Let's go through each one:

Step 1: Question it. When those negative thoughts start swirling through your head, you need to stop and ask yourself how true the thought really is. In many cases, the negative things aren't true or are maybe just partially true. When you're upset, it's easy to think the worst.

Stop and look at the negative thoughts that are haunting you the most. It can help to write them down and look at each one individually and ask the question, how true is this, really? What do the facts tell you?

Step 2: Say it. You can do this in a few ways and we

suggest you try several to see what works for you.

One of the most helpful things you can do for yourself is to share what happened and how you're feeling with people you know who will be supportive. Let them tell you that what the company did was totally unfair.

They can also help you with your Step 1 Questions by pointing out what's not true and reminding you of all the great things you did for the company.

It's important to choose wisely the person with whom to talk. Yes, sometimes you just need a bitchfest, but it's better if you can talk with a pal who can give you some ideas and get you on a positive path.

Saying what happened can be very very difficult, especially if you're feeling very sad and are full of shame, but sharing this with others is part of the healing process.

We've seen people push themselves to share with lots of people and post their stories on TikTok and other sites. Just be aware that not everyone will love that and you may have to deal with trolls who leave negative and hateful comments. You should also be careful about posting anything especially if you signed an agreement with the company when you left. Also, future potential employers might not be excited about hearing how you talk about your past job.

If you're not ready to share with your friends yet, you can start out by just saying what happened aloud. It may feel odd but saying your concerns and worries aloud can take away some of their power. When they're swirling around in your head, the words and emotions invoked can feel impossible to deal with, but when you speak the words aloud, you realize that they are manageable.

Another way to say it is to journal about it. You can just start typing or if you want to go old school, buy a physical notebook and grab a pen. Set a timer for 15 or 30 minutes. If you want to keep writing when the timer goes off, you can; otherwise, you're done for the day.

The goal is to write out any thoughts you have to help you process them. You don't have to make complete sentences, just spew out the words through your fingers and pen.

If you're stuck, here are some prompts you can use:

- What thought keeps repeating?

- What is bothering me/gnawing at me?

- Finish these sentences:
    o Something they said that keeps coming back is…
    o Something they did that I keep replaying is…

Getting through the stages of grief, anxiety, distrust, fear, and your shattered self-confidence can be a lot of work. And it may take more work than you can do by yourself, as sometimes it can be difficult to get outside our own heads and to "unfuck" ourselves, as Jill's husband says. If you find yourself struggling, this could be the time to speak to a licensed counselor or psychologist and possible medication referral. We all need assistance in certain situations and professional support may launch us ahead in ways we ourselves and our friends and family can't.

Laura's counselor was incredibly helpful when she was laid off, and she was glad she didn't wait to contact her. Laura had been beating herself up about what she should have done to prevent her job loss, but in reality, when she looked at the situation with the help of her counselor, it became clear that her efforts would not have made a difference. When Laura realized that, it was like a weight was lifted from her shoulders. Until that moment, she didn't understand how stressed she really was and that helped her to accept the situation and to move on more quickly.

Step 3: Rewrite it. This is your opportunity to rewrite the negative story that you're telling yourself. You have control over your story and you can choose a better story by replacing the negative messages with positive ones.

Instead of thinking, I'm no good and I lost my job, you can think instead:

That company wasn't a good match and I'll find a better place.

Or:

That job wasn't what I expected and there are better jobs for me out there.

Or:

The company changed direction and now I have an opportunity to do something I want to do.

We'll go into this in more detail in the future chapters. But for now, let's go back to Laura's example of how she felt shamed by the person who cut her contract to part-time. Laura wishes she had a book like this at the time because it would have made things much easier. If she had, this is how the steps would have worked for her.

Step 1: Question it. Laura had lots of negative thoughts running around in her head. Probably the most damaging were: I was so stupid to focus on this contract job; I should have taken the other contracts. And I should have known that this was going to happen. I'm really dumb.

If Laura had taken the time to question these thoughts, she would have realized that they were not really true. The facts showed that the company had not given any indication that they were even considering changes. All the messages they sent showed that they were happy with the current situation. And if Laura had taken on other contracts, then she would have been working way too many hours. So she realized not taking the other contracts was wise, not dumb.

Step 2: Say it. Laura felt so ashamed and embarrassed that she didn't tell any of her friends right away. If she had been able to talk about it, she would have felt so much better. They could have helped her to see that the manager said what she did so she didn't have to take the blame for not communicating earlier. Laura didn't talk to her friends though and spent weeks stewing about it and feeling worse and worse until she couldn't take it any longer and her emotions had to erupt to someone.

Step 3: Rewrite it. Laura could have changed the story to:

"The company shifted focus, and I get a chance to try something new."

"I can work with other companies that are aligned with what I like to do."

Focusing on these thoughts would have helped Laura get through the process quicker and with less pain.

What about you? How can you use the 3-step process now to help you to move forward?

Let It Go

It's easy for us to tell you in order to move on you must let go, but you can't do it for us. You have to let go for yourself. Ask yourself, why do I want to let it go? What do I have to gain by releasing my emotions and the pain?

Typically holding onto these thoughts and feelings is like walking around with lead weights on your shoulders. Every day this pressure makes it harder and harder to get things done and feel okay. If you feel that statement, then check out these ways to Let It Go.

Meditation. If you don't already use meditation, this could be a great time to start. You may think, oh I could never sit still or my mind loves to wander. One simple way to use meditation is to simply sit or stand or walk and force yourself to think of breathing. That's it. You know how to breathe, right? Inhale and exhale. Inhale and exhale and say in your mind "in" and "out" as you suck in that breath and let it back out. Focusing on these two words can make it easier to relax.

There are also some great apps available like Calm and Headspace that have paid and free versions, so they won't cost you a thing. Some yoga apps and programs also have meditation recordings to listen to, as does YouTube. Jill uses earbuds and listens to ocean waves crashing and binaural beats on the BrainWave app (a one-time fee that's around the cost of a cup of latte) when she meditates and also while she focuses on writing and editing books, since BrainWave also has settings for critical thinking and concentration and creativity.

One problem we hear from people who are new to meditation is that they say their thoughts keep interrupting so they give up. For most of us, thoughts will keep interfering and that's okay. Imagine putting up a buffer between you and your thoughts using breathing or repetitive words or sounds. When the thoughts push through, calmly push them back or imagine them falling to the ground. Don't give up because you can't stop the thoughts. Just keep breathing and bringing your mind to the present moment.

Another issue people have is the belief that they don't have time for meditation. It doesn't take an hour. You can meditate for ten minutes or two minutes or one minute. The important thing is to try it and see how it can work for you. And to do it consistently, even for one-minute each day.

Take Care of Yourself. One key thing when you are letting go after you've been dumped by your job is to figure out ways to take care of yourself. Think about it, if a friend of yours had just gone through what you've been through, wouldn't you tell them to be kind to themselves? You wouldn't berate them or make them feel shittier.

But we do that to ourselves all of the time. Instead, follow what you'd do for your bestie and treat yourself with compassion and kindness. And part of that is paying attention to your energy and making sure that you're scheduling time for whatever builds your energy. Exercising and focusing on strengthening your body can help you escape the negative thoughts and feelings. So go walk your dog, climb a tree or a wall at the gym, go to Pilates or kickboxing (and yes, you can mentally picture your ex-company's logo on the bag you are kicking), or throw a dance party in your living room. Move your body and release those feel-good endorphins.

You can also remind yourself that other things besides a job are important to you. Get out of your head and focus on the bigger picture. Get into nature. Go to church or temple. Escape into a book or movie, or visit a relative or friend you haven't seen in a while.

Whether it's watching cute puppy videos, listening to your favorite songs, having a sex marathon, or working in your garden, be sure to spend time doing what you love and this will have the ripple effect of making you feel better.

CHAPTER 3

Don't Go Into Armadillo Mode

DID YOU KNOW THAT when an armadillo gets hit by something or feels threatened it curls its head and tucks its tail and forms a ball, allowing only its thicker shell to be exposed to the outside world? It's like being in the fetal position inside of armor. We understand how that might sound appealing to you right now.

But the thing is, humans lack biological and physical armor. So we often try to create it with our attitudes, our energy, and by shutting down our hearts to things that have hurt us.

And when we get laid off or fired, we may feel the urge to squeeze into the tightest ball we can to ward off the outside world. But when we act like an armadillo, we aren't open to the kindness and help of others AND we keep all of the hurt energy and feelings inside our core or at the center of the ball we have formed. And holding onto all of that negative energy harms us.

Manage Fears

Why are we so afraid of what happened and what's to come? Why aren't we excited about the unknown and the opportunity to find something new that might be WAY better? Granted, some people are, but for most of us, our initial thoughts are mostly negative. (A recent study, as reported by the National Science Foundation, showed that 80 percent of the thoughts we have each day are negative and 95 percent of our thoughts are repetitive.) That's normal; it's your brain protecting you.

The amygdala is the old part of your brain that protected us when we lived in caves. It's the part that said, "Be careful, there could be a saber-tooth tiger." Fortunately for those of us living in the twenty-first century, there are no more saber-tooth tigers, but our brain still sometimes acts as if there are. The good news is that once we realize that's what our brain is doing, it's easier for us to deal with it calmly and rationally. We need to let that scared part of our brain know it's okay, that we are safe.

You have a couple of choices when it comes to fear. You can hide like an armadillo or you can stretch with your arms and open your chest and your eyes and take a look at what's really going on.

Let's go back to the 3-step model of Question, Say, and Rewrite and focus on how to question. Pick a scary thought that you want to question. Any thought that makes you anxious. Or use this one: I'll never get another job.

When you actually say these words aloud, even if they make your chest feel tighter, you realize that the words are not true at all. You know you'll get another job.

But maybe your brain protests: I'll never get another job as good as this one.

Does that feel more real to you, and closer to the truth?

Ask yourself, how true is the thought I'll never get another job as good as this one? Sure, it may feel like you're never going to get another job that's as good because you really liked what you were doing and thought the team was terrific and got a good salary and…and…and…

But really, is it reasonable to think that you'll NEVER be able to find another job that you like as much? Well, no, you're probably saying, but I'll miss the… Stop right there. All we want to do is look at this thought. If you're real with yourself, the answer is that it's probably not true.

Now think about how this thought makes you feel. Does it empower you to get out there and look for a great job, or does it make you want to sit on the couch and scroll through social media? If thinking that makes you feel sad, it's time to get rid of this thought.

Wouldn't it be great if we could just take it and dump it in the trash, like we do with unwanted things on our desktops? But our thoughts aren't as easy to delete. Instead, the space the repeated thought has grooved into our brain must be overridden by other, more positive thoughts (like reprogramming your internal mental software). What are ways you can turn around that thought I'll never get another job as good as this one so it makes you feel better or motivates you?

This is where step 3, Rewrite it, comes in. Instead of thinking, I'll never get another job as good as this one, you can believe:

- My next job could be even better.

- I can get a job that lets me do even more of something I really like.

- I can find other great teams to work with.

- I can find a job that pays more.

Add your own rewrites to the list until you find some thoughts that resonate with you and fill you with happiness or comfort. Then when your mind goes to that old negative thought, quickly stop it and say the words that make you feel better instead.

One way to help you do that is to write it out and put it up where you can see it, such as on your mirror, as a background on your phone's lock screen, or as your computer screen background. That way when the thought appears—and it will—then you'll be prepared to fight it.

Or you can try this cool mind override hack: When you start to hear the negative messages in your head say,

"STOP" or "CANCEL." That will interrupt the suckers and will halt the spiraling into negativity that makes you want to drown your sorrows. If you're by yourself, say the words aloud to break the chain of thoughts. Then do something physical, like a push-up or a butt wiggle or whatever your thing is. And/or you can stand up and turn around and say, "I'm going to turn this around." Sounds hokey, we know, but it works. Or you can pretend you're Taylor Swift and put your hands up and shake them while shouting, "Shake it off." Or you can make a pitching motion and imagine pitching that thought in the trash.

The point is, you can use words and thoughts to stop your reeling mind and then choose something more positive to think about. It won't be easy at first, but it will be worth it when you start feeling better.

The Power of Yet

Another way to help you to change the story in your mind is to use the word yet. When you say negative things to yourself change them to:

I don't have a job, YET.

I don't have a great LinkedIn profile, YET.

I don't have a kick-ass resume that shows how awesome I am...YET.

This simple change can help you move from stuck to focusing on actions you can take to get to a better future. But there are other tools you can use, too. For example...

One Question

Another thing that can make you feel better and get the momentum going toward your goals is asking yourself the daily single, repetitive question: What can I do today that my future self will thank me for?

Add the question to your other daily habits and ask yourself this question first thing in the morning as you're downing your coffee or Red Bull. What can I do today that my future self will thank me for? Chances are the answer is not: sit and play video games. (Unless, of course, you are or plan to be employed by Nintendo, Ubisoft, EA, Epic, or the like.)

This question—What can I do today that my future self will thank me for?—can stimulate you to push yourself to do things that may not be comfortable right now. For example, you may know you need to update your resume and Linkedin profile but it seems like too much work. When you remind yourself that in a few months you'll be glad you spent the time, it can help you to take action even when you don't feel like it.

Reach Out to Your Tribe

When we keep all of our stewing to ourselves and get stuck on the negative thoughts looping through our heads, we can start to believe them and are brought down emotionally and psychologically even lower. This is why it is so important to reach out to your friends, your mentor, your family, and even your dog, cat, or other critter who will listen to you and help you to feel better about yourself. (Animals are great at showing unconditional love.)

Odds are that someone in your circle of loved ones or acquaintances has been through exactly what you are going through. (And if for some reason you don't have anyone to talk to, reach out to us. Coaching people through employment situations is what we do.) Or, as Laura said, a professional therapist is also a good choice to provide a broader perspective than the weeds you currently are trying to whack through.

But maybe you are hesitating to reach out to anyone or to talk about what has happened to you because you are afraid. Let's talk about that.

One of the fears some people have is, oh shit, I have to tell my partner, my family, and my friends. What will they say? What will they think?

Normally our first thought isn't, I bet they're going to be happy and proud of me. No, our first thought is they're going to be so upset/furious/disgusted/pissed off/disappointed or (add your own here). We take the things that are worrying us and project onto others. Yes, they'll probably be just as shocked as you and will be upset. But think back to the three things you could be feeling about the situation. Your friends and family may react similarly. Their version could be:

1. You really messed up. You should have known or done something to avoid this.

2. Those bastards, they suck.

3. Thank goodness, I'm so glad you're not at that place anymore. They didn't treat you well and didn't deserve you and now you can get something better.

Responses 2 and 3 can help you move through this quicker as long as you don't get caught up in blaming your previous company for how bad they suck. Or get stuck in mentally questioning what your friend or family member thinks of you. For example, Jill agreed to take a job with a new company and resigned from her role at a place she had worked for more than a decade. Her partner at the time responded, "I can't believe you stayed at that place as long as you did with how they treated you." That stopped Jill in her tracks. She had mostly loved working there. Sure, it had its issues like every place did, but did that mean her partner thought she was stupid or made bad decisions in her life or didn't see things clearly?

Instead of questioning yourself if you get a number 2 or 3 response, reassure yourself that your loved one is being supportive and commiserating with you.

If the other person responds with number 1, that's when you might want to give them some time to process and start to go through the five stages of grief without them. Keep in mind that the loved one is going through the same issue with their brain trying to protect them. They could be spiraling into worrying about how you will both pay the rent, buy food, make your car payments, etc.

This is the time to be kind to yourself and kind to your loved ones, too.

Reach Out To Ex-Colleagues

When we go into armadillo mode, we might also shrink

from reaching out to other employees who are still at the company even though this is the right time to send a positive or neutral message to people letting them know that you're going on the next step in your journey and making sure you're connected on LinkedIn. After all, you don't know how long they're going to be there either. Staying in contact and banding together can be a great way to get a new job when they move to a new company (if you haven't found a company by then). Or maybe you can bring them to your company.

If you've thought about connecting with ex-colleagues but haven't, it could be because you feel shame and embarrassment.

Another excuse we've heard is that it's too late now. As in, I was let go two weeks ago (or two months ago) and it's too late to reach out to people. I should have sent them a message that day.

Not true.

Here's one reason why. On the day you found out, and for some time after that, you may have been in too much pain to say anything in a positive or neutral way. You may have needed to give yourself time.

If you can send something out right away, great, then do it. But if you're not sure you can send a message that doesn't sound pissed off or sad, then it's better to wait.

Yes, we've all heard exciting stories where someone left the company and sent a brutal email to the whole company, including the CEO, exposing their stupidity. Or someone live streamed themselves on TikTok while or shortly after they were being laid off so the whole world could see. This may sound like fun, but it is a bad idea. It is not going to help you or anyone else. And you may become infamous as the person who behaved badly in your industry, and this could make it difficult to get another job.

If you do really want to write down the reasons your company or boss suck, you can but NOT as an email. Just go ahead and type it out and file it away. Or text your best friend. Or even better, you can write on a piece of paper all of the reasons why your boss was a moron and why the company is in the toilet because of their stupid management mistakes and ass kissing. When you're all done, you can rip it into tiny pieces or light it on fire to help you to let go of those feelings.

Another thing that might stop you from networking with colleagues is concern that people might not message you back because they feel uncomfortable and don't know what to say. Yep, that could happen, but who cares? The fact is that some people you message will ghost you. It happens. Ignore them. The good news is that some people are happy to hear from you, and those are the people with whom you want to stay in contact.

CHAPTER 4

Come Out of Your Shell and Turning Leaving Into Learning

WE TALK ABOUT THE IMPORTANCE of letting go of the past job and not obsessing over it, but spending a little time thinking about it and deciding what you've learned from it will benefit you, especially as those bits of insight can determine what and how you go forward and make decisions.

For example, Jill worked as Chief of Staff for a CEO who wasn't super self-aware. Two VPs were scheduled to lead a workshop for the c-suite level customers. Just as the

VPs kicked off the workshop, the CEO of Jill's company walked to the front of the room and commandeered the whole meeting. After sixty minutes of him talking while the VPs stood aside and fumed and half of the customers left the room, Jill was completely flabbergasted. Afterwards, her CEO asked Jill, "What'd you think?"

What Jill really thought, she kept to herself. But she was honest when she said, "Did you see more than half of the room cleared out? What you said wasn't related to what this meeting was supposed to be about. The VPs are very unhappy."

They, the VPs, had left the room too so he couldn't check with them. But he said to Jill, "I told you when I hired you half your job is to save my ass. You should have made me stop."

"Yeah, right. In front of three hundred other executives. I don't think so. You'd fire me for making you look bad."

He eyed her for a moment before smiling and saying, "Next time pass me a note that says, 'Quit being an asshole.'"

The lesson from that experience that Jill took forward into future employment (yes, she ended up swiping left on that company a few months later) was to never take a job where half the job description is to save someone from themselves, especially if they can't read a room.

When you look back at what you've learned and examine your time with the company, it's important not to get stuck there or let your emotions get the best of you. Revisit for a moment and explore the areas that make you feel like shit and where you triumphed. In other words...

Look Back Briefly and Focus Forward

An important part of this exercise is to keep in mind that the old job was a stepping stone to the next part of your journey and your next job. This is NOT the time to beat yourself up. Instead this is a time to appreciate what you did get from it so you can use that in the future. Just like you can appreciate your years in college without wishing that you were still enrolled full-time in school. (Or maybe you do wish you were...but that's a different discussion.)

Here's how to look back briefly while focusing forward. Take a deep breath and let's get started. Ask yourself:

- What are the main things I learned from my last job?

- In what areas did I grow?

- What was most exciting about the job?

- What was most fun for me?

- Where did I feel stuck? Why is that?

- Looking back, what changes could I have made that would have made it better for me?

- What do I wish I had done more quickly?

- What do I wish I had avoided?

- Who did I admire and why?

- What did I learn about myself?

- What did I learn about working with others?

- How did that job affect what I want to focus on in the future?

- What do I wish had been part of that job?

Let's turn these answers into a roadmap for the future:
- What do I want to learn at my next job?

- In what areas do I want to continue to grow?

- What is important for me to get at my next job? (think about skills utilized, money and benefits, position level, work environment, etc.)

- What do I want to avoid at my next job?

- What kind of people do I want to work with?

- What kind of customers (internal or external) do I want to work with?

- What do I want to spend the majority of my time doing?

- What is important to me? Why?

Take this information to help you to picture your best next job. How would you describe it to someone else? Be as specific as possible. And think about the last question, "Why?" This is an important question because it can help you to uncover some more things that might be important to you.

And if you get stuck trying to answer, play an offshoot of Never Have I Ever by playing Never Again Would I Ever... (If you don't know the rules of the game, you literally list the things you would never again do. Really. It's that simple and can be played anywhere...or at least any place you are permitted to talk or think.)

Once you are certain what would make you swipe left in an employment situation, it makes it easier to determine what would make you swipe right (and hint: it is often the never again's opposite).

The struggle after leaving a job is real. But without struggle and change there is no growth. The job search can be a great way for you to learn about yourself, including what you're good at and what makes you cringe.

Time For A New Direction?

As you consider what you don't want to do, ponder what you DO want to do. Do you want to stay on the same path you were on or would you like to explore a new direction? While you are unemployed is a great time for you to look at different options. Right now some companies are talking about reducing headcount, and at the same time other companies are actively recruiting and expanding.

Use this opportunity as a chance to look at not only other companies but also other industries and other kinds of jobs. What other jobs would be related to your last job? How can you build the skills that employers are looking for?

Back To School Or Not?

One thing that can happen after being dumped by your company is you may ponder if more certification or a degree or advanced degree would be beneficial. Have you been wondering if additional schooling is right for you?

It may sound good, but don't jump in with both feet right away. Consider a few things first. The job descriptions that you're looking at may mention additional degrees, but are they listed as "Desired Qualifications" or "Required Qualifications"? If they're desired, you don't necessarily need those degrees as long as you bring other things to the job that they're looking for. Also, keep in mind that even though something might be listed as "Required," companies do make exceptions. They might not find anyone with enough of those "Required" qualifications so they might change them. (For example, we've seen jobs that ask for 10+ years experience and a master's degree but have such shit pay the company readjusts the requirements to fit the salary or vice versa when the desired applicants don't apply.) Or the company might look at other areas of your experience and say that it is equivalent. This is especially true if you know someone at the company and can get a referral.

Of course, the other big problems with getting additional degrees or even certifications are time and money. Do you seriously want to burden yourself with that much debt right now?

Laura and Jill do have advanced degrees and are big supporters of additional education WHEN it makes sense. At one point, Jill had to make the decision between taking an offered chair position at the university where she taught or give up her salary and teaching to pursue a doctorate. If she went the Ph.D. route, it would have taken her seven years or more to get to the place where she'd be offered a department chair position again. So she opted to stay in the workforce and go into academic management.

Early in Laura's career she was admitted to a prestigious graduate degree program and chose not to go when she realized how much the full-time program would cost. A few years later she started a part-time graduate program that her company paid for. It took her more than five years to earn the degree, but she was happy that she didn't have a huge bill when she was done.

If you do want an additional degree, you could do the same thing as Laura. Focus on getting the next job first and have them pay for all or part of it.

Another educational area that you should consider is certifications. You can get them faster and cheaper than a degree. They can also be very helpful if you're trying to make a career shift. For example, Google offers great online certification programs on topics such as Digital Marketing & E-commerce, Project Management, IT Support, and Data Analytics. You can go to Coursera.org to get more information and also find certificate programs and courses from some of the nation's top universities, like UPenn's Wharton School of Business, Yale University, and many more. Some certificate program fees are nominal and a small percentage of what you would pay for a degree.

Many companies are realizing that degrees are not as important as people's skills and abilities and recognize the value of certifications so it's worth it to check them out.

Even if you're not finished with your certificate, be sure to put it on your resume to show potential employers that you're working on it. And add it to your LinkedIn Profile (Coursera has links for LinkedIn to the certificates you earn through them so it makes them easy to add to your profile.)

How to Not Carry Past Baggage into Future Employment Relationships

We all carry baggage. Whether we like to admit it or not. We lug around weighty emotions like added appendages and invisible overloaded backpacks overflowing with experiences, skills, challenges, hopes, dreams, fears, things we like, things we hate, our insecurities and triggers, and past work trauma. The big question is, how much of that crap do you want to carry into your future employment?

Would you love to feel lighter and less encumbered by your emotions and employment history? Part of the way you can do that is by doing the Looking Back Briefly but Focusing Forward exercise. Delve into the questions, examine what you've learned, and then use that information to determine what you want at your next proverbial rodeo.

Say Goodbye

Letting go is not easy. The longer you were at a job, the more difficult it will be for you.

When you get to let go, you may want to jump right back into getting a new job, and for some of us, making sure we have a replacement paycheck ASAP is the most important thing. Even then, you want to make sure you really say goodbye to the old job. That may sound silly because after all they just said goodbye to you, but do you really feel closure?

A big mistake people make is to jump too quickly to the next job before closing out the issues from the old job. Just like dating, the problem with that is that you run the risk of getting into the same old shitty relationship.

William Bridges, author of *Transitions: Making Sense of Life's Changes*, has a simple model for change. The first part is Endings, the second part is the Neutral Zone, and the last part is New Beginnings. We may want to jump to the new beginnings, but first we need to close out that chapter of our lives. How do we do that? Think about what loose ends we still have. Some might be physical. Maybe you haven't sent back your badge or some other things that you need to do. Or maybe there is a box in your garage or closet with stuff you took out of your desk, cubicle, or office, when you were leaving and you haven't been able to go through it. The time to tackle that is right now. So, go, right this minute and tear open that box and go through that past-life shit.

You never know what you'll find...like maybe a business card that will lead to your next job opportunity or enough paperclips to create a replica of the TARDIS or maybe that tie or extra set of heels you kept in your desk "just in case."

Okay, so has the box been emptied or thrown away or repacked? Do you feel any closure or inspiration or surprise? (Hello, unremembered Starbucks gift card.)

The important thing here is to really say goodbye to the job. You are not going back and that's a good thing. If this has been a particularly hard breakup for you, you may want to find a way to make it more formal so you really feel like you are able to let it go. Because unless you can let it go, you won't be able to easily move ahead and get the next great job.

After Laura learned about the different stages of change, she made it a practice to say goodbye to things so that there would be room to say hello to the next adventure. When she moved from one house to another, she and her daughter walked into each of the rooms of the old house and said thank you for the memories and said goodbye.

You can do that for your job also. Thank it and say goodbye. That can be a quick thought or you might need a more specific goodbye. For example, you could write a note that says goodbye (of course don't mail it) or maybe you just blast "Goodbye To You" by Scandal while you dance and wave goodbye. Find a way that works for you so you can let go and put that job and company behind you.

After you've done that it's time to run into the Neutral Zone, which Laura calls the Zone of Confusion since feelings of uncertainty may attack you like mosquitos at dusk as you navigate through the swamp to find your next job. Give yourself the time and space you need to explore. Expect that it will be uncomfortable and see it as a necessary step to get you to where you want to be, which is the final stage, New Beginnings. That's when you start the job you want.

You Have The Choice

It may not feel like it right now, but you have the power to choose how you feel and react. You can choose to focus on negativity and uncertainty, or you can see things with hope and optimism.

When you're faced with a difficult situation like getting a job, you can focus on why you'll fail or you can focus on why you'll succeed. If you're not feeling positive right now, you might be wondering how you can do that. You can look at what has helped you be successful in the past.

For example, you can think about how you got your previous job(s) or just think in general about how you've been able to handle tough times when you didn't know what to do. You can also think about your strengths. For example, that you're good at learning new things. Or you can think about people you know who can help you. They may not be able to get you a job but they can give you advice. Thinking about these advantages can help you to move forward more positively.

Imagine Your Ideal Job

Now take your learnings and design your ideal job. Fold

a piece of paper into two columns or start two columns on an electronic document. Write down a list of all the things you want in the left column and all the things you don't want in the right column.

Of course, it would be difficult to get everything you want. Just like job descriptions, there should be requirements and things that would be the bomb, such as extra bennies. Review the list and choose the most important non-negotiables for you. Circle them or put them in bold. Those are the things you need to focus on in your job search. And now that you know what you need, let's talk about how to put yourself back out there.

CHAPTER 5

How To Get Back Out There

GETTING BACK OUT THERE to the job search is similar to swimming through all of those thousands of dating profiles. When you wade in and stick your face in the water, you hope to see brightly colored and lively fish—things that make you feel alive. But instead, you're surrounded by silt, murky water, and crappie minnows.

What can you do?

First, in your effort to get back out there, you need to update your image. That means...

Create a New / Updated Profile

Log into your LinkedIn account and let's make your profile stand out. Studies show that the average time a recruiter or company spends on a person's LinkedIn Profile is seven seconds. Yep. Not much time. So yours needs to stand out and stand out quickly. Here's how to do that.

Photo. Have you uploaded a great photo of yourself? If you haven't, take a headshot and put a face to your name so recruiters can see you.

LinkedIn Banner. That big rectangle that your photo sits on is called the LinkedIn Banner. Many people leave it blank. That's a mistake. With only seven seconds to capture someone's attention and tell them who you are, you must use that banner space to your advantage. In Canva, you can use a template for that banner. Write words in it or put in easily recognizable symbols or whatever you think screams you to potential employers.

For example, Jill's banner has a solid color background and then uses the palette of red, yellow, blue, and green for the labels of what she does: author, book coach, higher education consultant, entrepreneur, editor, etc. That way people have an instant understanding without reading all of the rest of the words on her profile.

Headline. Under your photo is a short headline (120 characters max.) Instead of focusing on a job title, mention your specialty or what you bring to the table. For example: Super-star pharmaceutical salesperson with a $40 million+/ annual territory.

When writing your headline keep in mind your audience.

Are you targeting recruiters or headhunters? Corporate HR? Write something that will attract attention from your target audience and help you get an interview.

Summary. This is where you can expand on the headline and provide more concrete details of who you are as an employee or a boss or an entrepreneur. The summary space gives you 2000 characters to focus on what you bring to any job (don't focus this area on your past experience).

For example, As an information security analyst at a five-hospital system, I manage the day-to-day flow of information and focus on database management. My job ensures critical computer systems, medical files, and patient histories remain active and never fail. I focus on safety but also the most cutting edge technology.

Experience. When you focus on the experience you've had at each job, don't do a cut and paste from your resume. LinkedIn allows you to be as long-winded as you want (though keep in mind people's attention spans have been shrinking for decades). Best practices here use two to four bullet points of the most kick-ass accomplishments and make the use of active verbs to show what you did in each position. Focus on initiatives taken and results delivered.

Skills. LinkedIn allows you to pick your top skills, though actually not just your top ones, but 50 things in which you are skilled. Use that. Choose all 50. Don't be shy. And then ask your friends and family to endorse you for that skill. The more endorsements the better to show you rock.

Connections. It may seem obvious to say "make friends" on LinkedIn but connections are everything on the platform. If you are new to LinkedIn, start with the people you know and push the connect or follow buttons. Most nice people, if you connect to them, will connect or follow you back. Include a little note as to why you are connecting, if you don't know the person IRL. If you feel the need to build out your connections, set a goal for yourself to ask one person or five people each day to connect with you. You never know where your next job will come from.

Recommendations. Recommendations are very important because they show the working world who thinks you're awesome or the GOAT. :) The best way to get people to write recommendations for you is to ask them, but couch it in this way: "I would love to write a recommendation for your LinkedIn Profile and since you know what I'm like to work with, will you write me one, too?" This usually works like a charm.

Add Visuals and Posts. The LinkedIn community thrives on original articles, reposts and opinions on published materials, video content and more so be sure to post on your profile and to comment on others' posts. If you have a YouTube page, you can connect it to your profile.

Understanding Analytics and AI

We live in a time where your resume gets seen by AI (Artificial Intelligence) or RPA (Robotic Process Automation) before it ever gets to a human (and if the AI or RPA deems it not a fit, your resume never may be seen by a human). That's the reality and sometimes that sucks.

And what that means is resume writing becomes a game of How Can I Beat the System. The first step in doing that is to customize your resume to the job description. That doesn't mean to fabricate or exaggerate. It does mean to make sure your resume includes the buzzwords or keywords found in that job description and that you write them exactly as they are in the description. For example, if the job description mentions business to business sales experience and that's what you have, be sure to write it that way on your resume (don't write b2b as it is commonly abbreviated as AI doesn't recognize words when they are misspelled or shortened versions of what it has been programmed to search for).

Also, many AI or RPA "readers" cannot accurately read some resume formats. Most can read a simple, clean, and plain Word document. If you use fun formatting or text boxes, AI systems may not be able to read them correctly or pull the information from them to pass the information on to the human recruiter.

So it is best to use clear headings and simple language, like Summary, Professional Experience, Education, Certification, and Skills on the Word document.

Before You Hit Submit

Once you have a version of your resume completed, send it to a trusted friend, family member, or even hire us to review it. Having a second set of eyes on it will ensure that you spelled everything correctly, the resume is jargon-free and easy to understand, and that what you wrote speaks to the requirements of the types of jobs to which you will apply.

You may also want to ensure that the version you

are sending to a company has the necessary keywords embedded into your resume in a natural fashion. And that you have a strong cover letter, if one is necessary for that particular company. (Many companies no longer require them or make it impossible to include one when they are using corporate recruiting software systems.)

And once you've ensured whatever you've cut and pasted into their form or is on the resume you are going to upload is polished and professional and error-free, then feel free to hit submit.

Then the waiting begins and if it all goes well, you'll get an email from the recruiter or hiring manager asking to set up a call. When you see that, you may feel a burst of joy or a bit of relief, like Thank God, someone is interested in me.

CHAPTER 6

Interviews: How to Shine Bright Like a Diamond

Think of an Interview Like a First Date

Then it is preparation time, with research and decisions to be made. First the research. Jump on your computer and start sleuthing on the company, the recruiter or hiring manager, and find out everything you can. Regarding the company, look at the annual reports to get a snapshot of how the company is doing financially, what their values are, and if they have a sustainability statement (if this matters to you). Search their website for information of interest to you that you can also use during the discussion with the recruiter, manager, and the team (if you make it to that level of interviewing).

Does your potential manager play golf or have a dog on her social media profile? Does the company support a sports team that you love? Were they recently in the news in a way worth talking about, as in "I'd love to work at a company that values the local community so much that they fund the food bank or give their employees 40 hours of volunteer time each year."

The research you do of the company also helps you formulate intelligent questions to ask about the role, the work, and the organization itself. And having questions to ask makes you look curious, engaged, and prepared. (More on possible questions coming up in the next chapter.)

And then once you've snooped around and taken some notes on the company and the people you will be talking to, figure out what you are going to wear to make your best first impression—since you only get one.

When you prepare for a first date, you most likely dress to impress after showering, and you fix your hair and brush your teeth, right? You want the other person to think you look good and smell nice. Well the same goes for a first interview with a company or a company representative. You want to show up in a way that makes you look well-groomed and professional.

What that means is determined by the company and the industry in which you are interviewing. For example, the high tech industry used to laugh at potential employees who interviewed in coats or ties. A button down shirt or a polo and jeans or chinos was just fine for high tech.

Similarly, Amazon Corporate sends its prospective employees advice to dress casual for their initial video interviews as they promote a casually-dressed culture in-office. (For visiting customers, especially those abroad, the expected attire is more business formal.)

But if you are interviewing for a sales job where you know you are expected to look "high-end" then make sure your suit is cleaned and your shirt is pressed so that you make them say, "Wow" instead of "Whoa."

Preparation

Of course, when you're preparing for the interview, be sure to thoroughly check out the website and all recent stories about the company. Commenting on some things you learned can be seen as positive by the interviewer.

Another reason you want to do that is to help you get clear about what to focus on during the interview. Remember that the person interviewing you has probably just glanced at your resume, if they've looked at it at all. Your job is to look at the job description and information about the company and show them why you're the best candidate.

Just because something is listed on your resume, doesn't mean that they noticed it. Or if they did see it maybe they didn't realize the importance of it.

Part of your job in the interview is to find out their pain points and clearly explain how you can help them. It's really helpful to come prepared with some stories about how you've successfully addressed the problem in the past. Especially since many interviewers will ask you questions something like:

- Tell me a time when you had to do something difficult. What was it and how did you do it?

- Describe a time when you had to present information. How did you prepare and what was the result?

- Can you talk about a time when you had to learn something new? How did you do it?

Be prepared for questions like this by having examples ready. Look for ways to connect it to their pain points for this job. For example, you could tell a story about how you quickly learned something new. You could then say that you'd use similar skills to get up to speed as quickly as possible in the new job because you know how important it would be for them to have someone able to step up.

If the interviewer doesn't ask any questions looking for specific stories then find ways to add your examples to your answers.

Take Charge of The Interview

Many people underestimate the purpose of the interview process. Interviews are to help the company decide who they want to hire AND they should also help you decide if

Interviews: How to Shine Bright Like a Diamond

this is the right fit for you. It's a two-way street, not a one-way alley.

Before the interview, go back to your ideal job list and look at your non-negotiables and most important areas. Think about how you can ask questions that will help you to get a better understanding and make the right decision.

Here are some other things you can ask about:

- What's the best part about working here?

- What does success look like in this position? How is that measured?

- What is your management style? (If you're talking with the person who would be your manager). What is the leadership style of senior leaders?

- What are the main values of the company and how do those show up? (This could be a place where you reference what you found on the website. You could say, I understand that your company values teamwork and customer focus. How does that show up in this position?)

- What doesn't work well in this company? Can you give some examples?

- Why did the last person in this position leave?

If they say that the best thing about working there is that you're treated like family, be careful, since many families are super dysfunctional.

Ask your interviewer what brought them to the company and what keeps them there. You can also ask them what they like best about working for the company. Of course, recruiters will always say something cheery and positive because that's their job. It's much better if you can have the opportunity to talk with people who would be on your team. Their answers will be much more interesting, especially if you are left with them without any management around. Pay attention not just to the words but also to the tone. How long is the pause before they tell you why they like the job? Do they really have to think about it?

During interviews, always ask why the last person left. If the last person is still in the company and has been promoted, that's a great sign. That could indicate future opportunities for you. If the last person quit or was fired, pay attention to how they phrase it. What do they say about the person? If they say negative things about the person that could make you wonder if they will do the same about you. Another red flag is if different people say different things about why the person left. You'll also want to compare what they say with what you want. If they say the last person quit because he didn't like the hours or the travel or the reporting structure, you should consider if that could bother you in a few months.

It's also important to show up for the interview feeling your best. Even if you really need the job, you don't want the interviewer to hear your desperation. Take some time before the interview to center yourself and think about all the great things you could bring to the job and why they'd be lucky to have you decide to join them.

Think about your energy. You want to show up energetic and ready. If you have a video interview and have been sitting at your desk all day, it's time to get up, go for a quick walk outside, do a few jumping jacks or stretches or do something that will pump up your energy.

Think about what you do right before the interview. Do you have your head down, checking your phone? In an interesting study, Amy Cuddy, a Harvard researcher, found that even just two minutes of making yourself small (leaning over to check your phone) can make you feel less confident and two minutes of taking up more space (head up, shoulders back) can make you feel more confident. You can check out her TedTalk on Ted.org to get her views on how your body affects your confidence.

How To Address the Question of Why You Were Let Go

Preparing to interview for a new job can bring back all the anxieties and nervousness of when you first lost your previous job. After all, what do you say when they ask why you left your old job? Instead of worrying about it, plan for it. You know that this is a standard question that tends to come up in most interviews so be prepared.

First, get comfortable in your mind about what the story is. Then decide how you're going to spin it. Of course you should always tell the truth but you don't need to tell them everything. That's not necessary and they don't expect to hear the whole story. Normally, it's a much better idea to have a short simple answer prepared.

Lesa Edwards, Master Resume Writer, Certified Job Search Strategist & Career Coach at Exclusive Career Coaching, recommends that you think of the first interview like a first date. Tell the truth. Just not the whole truth.

One of her clients had previously tried a canned response to the question about why she left saying that she wanted a new challenge, but the interviewer pressed her for more information. This was a situation where the employee had a very difficult time with the manager and had been terminated.

Lesa Edwards helped her to craft a message that explained that there were no HR systems in place to support her when hiring a new employee and she was concerned that the lack of HR systems and processes exposed the company to legal issues. Even though she had been successful in parts of her job that made her uncomfortable and she didn't want to be in that position again. That was all true and helped to explain why this position she was applying for would be a good fit.

A big red flag for interviewers is if you start saying negative things about your past company or boss. Even if you worked for someone who was too stupid for words, you can't say that. The interviewer could think that you were a disgruntled employee at the previous company and you might end up being disgruntled there also.

It's better to keep it neutral and focus on the job and the company, not on you.

Barbara Limmer, Professional Career Coach and Consultant, suggests depersonalizing what happened and stating the business condition under which you were laid off.

You can say things like:

- There was a reorg in the department and several jobs, including mine, were part of the reduction.

- Like many other companies, there was a push to lower expenses and my job was affected.

- Or even, I was the last person hired in my department so when cuts needed to be made, I was the first person sent out the door.

This can be followed up with you saying why you're interested in this job and how great a match it is for your skills and interests in A, B, C, and D. This quickly answers the question and brings the focus back to the job you've applied for.

If you were let go due to a performance issue, you need to say what it was about that job that didn't speak to your specific skills. Be as specific as possible because they will fill in the blanks with things that may not be true, such as personality conflicts or other red flags.

You also don't want to sound too cheery because that could come across as though you're trying too hard. Don't say things like, "I lost my job but that's okay because now I've been able to spend more time on my hobby of yodeling." They certainly don't need to know that and may think you're being flippant.

Once you pick an answer that you like, try it out. Yes, actually say it aloud a few times, in front of a mirror or your phone camera on selfie mode. How does it sound? Do you think you sound confident and relaxed or do you sound upset? It's also a good idea to record yourself and play it back since it's hard to know how you sound when you're saying it. Pay attention to your tone and your facial expressions. Do you take a deep breath in at the beginning or grimace at the end? If you're nervous about how you're going to come across, it can help to have a friend practice with you and record your answers.

Keep practicing until you feel like you can calmly respond without wanting to scream.

Talking Too Much or Too Little

During interviews, like on first dates, we may be nervous and nerves or anxiety may cause us to act differently than we do in our day to day lives. Have you ever met someone for a date or at a party or in a coffee shop and you made a comment or even said a number of sentences and found yourself thinking, OMG, why did I say that?

We've all done it. We've tripped over words, used the wrong one to try to articulate what we mean, or said something we wished we didn't.

Or maybe you wished you would have said more, when asked a question or said something in response to a comment. While walking away we sometimes think, oh, that would have been a more clever response, and kick ourselves for not coming up with it sooner.

We do the same things during interviews. You've prepared and prepared and prepared and suddenly you're asked the question you damn well know the answer to and you said something you totally aren't expecting to come out of your mouth, so then you either clamp your mouth shut or get verbal diarrhea, spewing words to get at the heart of what you meant to say.

All the while thinking, idiot, idiot, idiot. Why'd I say that?

Law enforcement officers—who are trained in interview tactics—are taught that if there is a lot of silence people get uncomfortable and fill in the silence. And that's what you want to avoid doing during a job interview.

And this is why rehearsing your answers to the most common questions is so important and to have a list of your own questions at the ready so when there is a lull in the interview, you can ask an intelligent question and then be quiet and let the recruiter or hiring manager fill in the ensuing silence.

Don't be Afraid, Ask for What You Need or Want

During the interview process, one thing we need to gauge is when it is a good time to speak up about what you want or need in a new role. Initial interviews are often about listening to what the job entails, what the company culture is like, and then asking questions that make you look like you've done your research, are thoughtful, and will be a courteous team player.

But understanding the crux of the role and how things will be structured is essential to comprehending if the job will be a good fit for you. So if things like a flexible work schedule or remote work or one day a week WFH are important to you, do not be afraid to inquire about that during the interview process.

We cause many problems for ourselves when we make assumptions about how a situation or people will be instead of finding out the facts. For example, we may be excited at the possibility of working with this particular manager or executive and want the job based on that. But you may not know that that manager travels for her job ninety percent of the time and because of that she gives her teams a lot of autonomy and they rarely see her or work directly with her.

Or maybe the job requires you to work with team members in other parts of the world so you will be required to get on video calls or answer the phone at not normal business hours. It would be better to know that going into the job than being surprised on your first week of work with, "Hey, your workday starts every day with a five a.m. meeting with the team in the U.K."

Work as a Team Towards Common Goals

One mindset mistake we see people make is thinking that the recruiter and the hiring manager are your enemies or an obstacle you have to conquer in order to get to the prize of the job you want. When you think of them this way, the energy you emit towards them is very different than if you think of them as potential teammates of yours with whom you are working towards a common goal.

The job of the recruiter and/or hiring manager is to find and hire the best person to fulfill a role (because this makes them look good and makes their lives easier). Your job, as a candidate, is to help them easily understand why you are that person and how you will make their lives better by utilizing your skills, experience, talents, etc. to be a leader and someone who is a pleasure to work with.

Basically your goals are the same. You want the job and the chance to shine and grow and kick ass doing what you love to do. They want to find someone for the role who wants to do just that.

That's why showing camaraderie and courtesy is so important. And once you have the interview, send a thank-you email, thanking the recruiter or hiring manager for the time and for the opportunity to interview for X role. Reiterate why you want to work for the company and what you see as your added value, and tell them you look forward to talking to them further.

The ideal situation is that they give you a timeline for when you'll hear back and that they follow through. But that isn't always the case.

Rejection and Ghosting Are To Be Expected

Just like in dating, rejection and ghosting are common. It sucks, but it is the truth. With hundreds if not thousands of people applying for a single job—let's be real—the odds are stacked against everyone. That's why it is important to network on LinkedIn and IRL, to use those keywords to get past the AI and RPA, and to make yourself shine as someone who writes thank-you emails and follows through if you are asked for more information about anything during your interview.

And when you are rejected, breathe deeply and remind yourself that it wasn't the right fit or that something happened that was out of your control. (Some companies have interviewed a lot of people the last few months only to have the requisitions for the jobs themselves cut by corporate. Once again making it a case of it's not you, it's them.)

Remind yourself again that the rejection may not have a lot to do with you. It could be that someone with many more years experience applied, or someone who is internal to the company and known (as opposed to you, the unknown), or someone who is close friends with the hiring manager. Again, a company swiping left on your application may not be a direct effect of your resume or skill set.

But rejection of any kind sucks. And we feel like it is almost worse when it is the ghosting kind, since that feels like a loose end, right? You apply, interview, and then get radio-silence. Are they still thinking? Has the search process been put on hold? Did they hire someone else? Did they ax the position entirely?

It can be frustrating not to know.

If after a reasonable time, such as a week or two if they told you'd hear back by then, you've heard nothing, feel free to write a very polite email to the recruiter or hiring manager saying you would like an update. And once again, thank them for their time.

If you still get no response, it's best to shake off the disappointment and tell yourself you really didn't want to work with people who ghost anyway and move on.

CHAPTER 7

How to Know When You Should Swipe Right

CONGRATULATIONS! YOU'VE MADE IT through a few rounds of interviews and have received at least one offer. But how do you know if it's the job for you and you should swipe right?

By now you should know all about the company and its values. You've talked to the recruiter and the hiring manager and maybe even part of the team or someone from HR. You've probably looked at what the pay scale is for this job within your industry and you've considered the company's benefits and what they might mean to your life.

But are you jumping for joy or is something bothering the back of your mind or are you looking at the offer and feeling disappointed?

Getting Noticed

It's easy to get excited when you get any interest at all even if it may not be a good fit. You're just happy that someone noticed you and wanted you through the series of interviews and now has said they want to hire you.

But keep looking and don't stop looking until you have the signed offer letter. There's a natural tendency to slow down a job search when you get a first or second interview at a company but DON'T. Just because they're interested in you doesn't mean it's the right fit for you. Keep looking.

And even if the job feels right and they tell you that you're the best candidate and you have the job, don't believe it until you get the written job offer. They might love you but suddenly the budget is cut and the department can't hire anyone for that position.

Even when you do start a job, it's okay to keep things open. Laura has talked to people who started a job and then realized it was not what they expected and they've wondered if it's okay to quit and take another job. If that's true for you, warm up the other leads and keep looking.

Now don't jump too quickly. Laura remembers one job she had where she had lunch with her new boss on the first day and at the end of lunch wondered if she had made a big mistake. She decided to give it a little more time and after a few weeks she realized it was a great job and she stayed there for years.

Red Flags

We know them, we see them, and we ignore them. Why? Because humans can be stupid. But seriously, we ignore red flags because we often hope that things will get better—or that maybe we misunderstood if we see/hear some concerning things during the interview process.

But guess what? Often your gut (and intuition) are correct. And those things that were a bit of a red flag don't get better. Just like meeting someone for a coffee date and seeing them be nasty to the barista, red flags during an interview are messages that you need to pay attention to.

Always look for online reviews on sites such as Glassdoor and Indeed. You can expect that even great companies will have some low reviews. You're looking for trends, especially in recent reviews. A company that may have been great last year could have gone through some major changes and it may suck to work there now. So be on the lookout for recent ratings of upper management, what people have said about the job interview process, and how much time everything takes.

The way the job is described tells you a lot about how unreasonable their expectations may be. Here are some phrases to watch out for:

- Work hard, play hard (you're going to be expected to work a lot of hours)

- Startup culture (you're going to work crazy long hours)

- Fast-paced or high-pressure (they don't have enough people and are probably disorganized)

- Flexibility needed (meaning you need to work crazy long hours and on weekends)

- We're a family (you're going to be underpaid)

- Wear a lot of hats (your role won't be clearly defined and you'll be doing 2 or 3 jobs)

RUN! RUN! RUN! Unless that is the kind of all-encompassing work life you want.

Other phrases that should make you get out of there as soon as possible:

- We've had a hard time finding the right person. (When companies are seeing hundreds if not thousands of applications for a single opening, finding the right person shouldn't be that hard. Come on, people!)

- We want people who will go the extra mile. (Does that mean you may have to get your boss' coffee as well as take minutes during a meeting...even if that isn't in your job description?)

You should also be concerned if the job description

is too vague or if the recruiter says they are determining the scope of the job based on the applicant they hire and the person's skills. Companies should have a clear idea of exactly what they need and how this position fits into the team and into the whole.

This also brings up another interesting Red Flag issue regarding their questions. If their questions tend to mention similar issues then there's an excellent chance you're going to deal with it.

For example, if the questions are something like:
- Describe a time when a team member was difficult and you had to deal with it.

- Tell about a situation where you had a difference of opinion with another employee. How was that resolved?

Those two questions would make us wonder what the previous issues were and how that would affect the job.

Let's assume that the job you're interested in doesn't have any of those red flags. Let's talk about what happened during the interview process. How did they act when they talk to you? Did they sound super stressed and always busy? Maybe it is them or maybe the culture is high pressure and doesn't have enough resources. Laura remembers an interview at a company where the hiring manager was late to the interview and then got upset when she couldn't find a free conference room to meet in. She muttered about how crazy it was there. Laura had heard that this was a challenging environment and the interview confirmed it.

She didn't end up working there.

We've also had friends who have had interviews scheduled only to have the interview date and time change when the hiring manager suddenly was sent on a business trip. The follow-through of the company and the hecticness of the schedules and the environment need to be considered carefully.

If you went for in-person interviews, did you look around the reception area and the work areas? How did the employees look? How were they interacting with each other? Did they look stressed or did they look calm? Even if your job would be working from home, is this the culture you want to work in?

Don't dismiss red flags just because you want a job. You need to look for any red flags and then objectively review them to see the potential effect.

You know that example Jill gave back in the beginning of being forced from a job when the organization she worked for went under? Well, there's more to that story. A lot more in fact. At the same time all of that was going down, she started an executive master's degree program and one of the requirements was that all of the students had to be in management positions during the course of the study. You know, so they could do real-life stuff with the book learning.

Except, as we said, her organization shut its doors so Jill was not a big cheese any more. She felt more like a holey swiss and she struggled with having part of her identity suddenly ripped from her. So she took the first management job that came along even though her intuition yelled, "RUN!" from the offer. (The interviewing manager seemed a bit abrasive, like she was trying to be nice when she wasn't. And the office environment felt strained.) But Jill said okay to being their publications manager anyway.

But do you know what happens when you feel like the universe is bitch-slapping you and demanding NO and you do it anyway?

It takes very little time to hit bottom.

In Jill's case, it took about 90 days. In those three months, Jill's husband collapsed and ended up in the hospital, her adopted grandmother in Texas died from smoke inhalation in a fire and Jill needed the week off as she planned the memorial, her boss repeatedly took credit for all of the work that Jill did that won accolades from the c-suite and blamed her for all of the work the boss did that wasn't up to par (which is when Jill understood the nasty things her colleagues said about the woman), Jill tripped over her new puppy and fell down a flight of cement stairs and sprained five toes on her right foot and her knee and was put on crutches, and then during the final week of her employment with the organization, her paternal grandmother died so Jill needed to fly back to Pennsylvania for the week. It was at this time, in the CEO's office, that Jill acknowledged that she never should have taken the job in the first place. That she only did so out of panic so she could stay in the grad program.

Instead of panicking like Jill and learning lessons the super hard way, you could keep reading and learn how to deal with the break-up before you jump back into the work-relationship pool.

Keep Your Options Open

Some interview processes may take a long time. Even if you think you find the right job, don't stop looking or interviewing for other positions. It's easy to feel so great about a job possibility that you decide to slow down on your search. But jobs can easily fall through and no matter what they say, don't stop looking until you get the signed contact.

An added bonus about continuing to look and interview at other companies is that it can help you to show up with the right mindset. If you have decided that this is THE ONE and YOU MUST HAVE THIS JOB that could add a lot of stress to the interview process. Instead, if you know that there are other possibilities, it's easier to relax.

This can also be used as part of your negotiation strategy. If the interview process is going on and on for job A and job B looks like they're about to make an offer, you can mention it to job A in a nice way. You can say, I'm really interested in this job and know I could be a great addition to the team and I'm wondering what the timeline is. Of course, I have been applying at other jobs and there is another one that is close to making a decision. I would much rather take this job so I want to see where we are in the process.

Stop talking and see what they say. Don't give them any other information about the job, just repeat that you'd much prefer this job. This could give them FOMO and have them move a little quicker. Or they could say that it's still going to take them a while to make a decision.

If they are interested in you they may say, let us know

if you get another offer. If you do get an offer from job B, you can let job A know that you have received another offer but you would really like to work for them and give them a DEADLINE to let you know in writing that they want to hire you. If not, thank them very much and take job B.

Get the Best Salary

We cover this in detail in our book, *Increase Your Income: 7 Rules For Women Who Want To Make More Money At Work.* But here are some pointers:

Don't be the first to state a salary number. If they ask what salary you're looking for, turn it around and ask them, "what is the salary range for this job?" In many cases, they will tell you the range and then you just need to let them know that your salary requirements are in the range.

If they say a really low salary and way below what you want, let them know that that salary is much lower than what your research has shown for similar positions and ask them why that is. (Of course, you did do salary research to get a range before interviews.)

If you can put off a salary discussion, it can help you because it gives you the opportunity to show why you're the right person for the job. That way, if the salary is a little lower then what you're looking for, they might be willing to negotiate because they've already decided that they want to hire you.

When you do get the offer, ALWAYS ask for a higher salary. Even if it's a great salary, there is often some wiggle room. And even if there is no additional money, asking for more lets them know that you believe you are worth more which could help you get a bigger raise in the future.

When they offer you the job and tell you the salary, thank them and reinforce why you're the best candidate (I'm excited about joining the team and helping them to do X). Then pause and say, "Is there any flexibility?" Stop talking and wait for them to respond. They may not know, especially if you are talking with the recruiter. Then say, "Would you please check and let me know?" Thank them again.

Many people are nervous about asking for more money, but we have heard so many stories about people asking and making more money. If you don't ask, you won't get anything.

Is This the Right Job?

Let's face it, there is no perfect job. There are great jobs and then there are good jobs that you can make better. This whole process is to help you get the next right job for this part of your career journey.

When you look at your ideal job and your non-negotiables, ask yourself what will make you happiest/most relieved/excited now and for the next six months to a year. Swipe right on the best job for you for right now and then you can decide what's next for you.

CHAPTER 8

Create the Work Relationship of Your Dreams

MOVING TO A NEW COMPANY is like moving to a new city. In most cases, no one knows you there and you have a chance to start fresh. Of course, some industries are smaller than others and some people may have heard about you from colleagues they've worked with so be prepared for two degrees of separation or less in certain industries.

But regardless of how small your industry, you have the opportunity to choose how you show up at *this* job. Close your eyes for a moment and picture your best self on the first day at work. How are you dressed? How do you feel? How will you act and speak in meetings and with your boss and teammates?

How will your way of being build on what you've already done? What will be new and different? Remember all of those questions we asked you to answer a few chapters ago, including the question about what you would have changed at your old job? Well, now's your chance to do just that, to rock the good stuff and to never again repeat the mistakes. Use those lessons you've learned to be the most awesome you can be at what you do.

Of course don't feel like you have to change everything and certainly not all at once. What is one main thing that is important for you to change (or not do) and what small things can you do every day to show up that way and reinforce the image you want to project? For example, if you want to show up as more confident, how will that manifest in your emails?

Be specific about how you want to show up and how you want to interact with others. Like dating someone new, this is your chance to make any impression you want. Jill worked with a program manager once who, from the day she started, referenced her previous company. As in, "Oh, at X we did it this way," or "I never had to do that in my job at X."

Yep, it was annoying for those around her from the get-go. But it was also a reminder of what NOT to do at a new job. So when we say start fresh, think about what you do and don't do, but also consider the lessons you've learned from previous colleagues and managers. All around us are good work and life examples of what to do and not do. This is one way to create the work relationship of your dreams.

But maybe through the past employment experiences you are on the fence about saying yes to a full-time corporate gig again. You feel shy about opening your heart to a company or feel like you've been burnt too badly, and maybe too often. We totally get that.

If that's you, have you considered self-employment? Self-employment takes many forms: entrepreneurship, temporary work, contracting, freelancing, and being a member of the gig economy. (And many of these things you can do as a side hustle even if you've taken that full-time employment position as a way to make extra cash.) Let's take a moment to consider why you may want to do some of your own things.

Self-Employment, Temporary, Project, and Freelance Work

Jill's book (published by Routledge) called *Creating a Freelance Career* provides a deep dive into self-employment. But for our purposes we will skate across the surface of this type of work because while you're looking for a new job, you may want to consider taking on some short-term projects, both to focus on your skills and keep them sharp and to make some extra money so you can pay the rent or mortgage.

Self-employment lets you be your own boss, set your own hours, do work that you love, choose the type of work and what clients you want to work with, and some of it you can do from anywhere. (Just in case you hear the open road calling your name.)

So many websites are geared to finding short-term project work (or contracts) in all kinds of industries and skills, for example, coding, project management, writing, editing, illustration, graphic design, proofreading, video editing, and so much more. If you want to find this type of work, where you do a set thing for a negotiated amount of pay, you can check out websites like freelancer.com, fiverr.com, flexjobs.com, communo.com, and upwork.com, just to name a few. Some of these sites are free and some have costs involved. If you start talking with any prospective clients on these sites make sure you STAY on the platform, as that's your only protection from scammers. And remember when you get contract work, if you make over $600 doing any number of contracts (individually or combined) you are responsible for claiming the money as income and paying taxes on it when you file the following year.

When Laura got unexpectedly laid off she was the sole breadwinner for her family and needed a paycheck quickly. She found a temporary contract position with a great company for 6 months (not the contract from an earlier story). The downside was that she had to pay for her own medical coverage, but the upside was that the pay was very good since it was a temporary position. (Pay for contracting positions is often higher per project or hour than a full-time position since the company doesn't have to shell out money for benefits and taxes—but you do.) That contract gave her time to find her next long-term position. She had not considered a contract position before that but it was the right choice for her then.

Maybe you want to use this time to explore different avenues, and it's the right time to do temp or contract work. Doing temp and contract work can also help you realize what it is you really love to do...or not.

Entrepreneurship

We've focused the majority of this book on how to handle a lay-off or firing and how to heal, and then how to find and land a full-time job at an existing company, but maybe that's not your ideal work situation. Maybe after working for The Man, you'd decided it's not for you. Could this be your chance to become an entrepreneur and build a hobby into a way to pay your bills. Do you have an idea you've always wanted to turn into a viable product or business? Have you considered working for yourself, but were hesitant to take the leap? But now that the universe has bitch-slapped you into unemployment, maybe now is the time to step up to the challenge.

But we'll be honest. Entrepreneurship and running your own business isn't for the faint of heart as the whole shebang rests solely on your shoulders (unless you recruit your BFF or colleague to launch the start-up with you). Successful entrepreneurs/business owners know how to manage, market, and sell in addition to handling their social media accounts, find and advertise to their customers plus oversee customer relations, manage their websites, do their own bookkeeping and much more—unless they surround themselves with others who can do those things by outsourcing the work. But then that means having money to pay for the contractors or staff who can handle the specialty work.

Both Laura and Jill are entrepreneurs, and they've both done freelance and contract and full-time work as they built their businesses. One of Jill's friends who runs an award-winning health app, walked dogs and pet and house sat for years while taking her concept and game from idea to full-fledged product. It was years before she could put herself on payroll, but now her app has been adopted at hospitals and rehabilitation centers and earned an endorsement from the U.S. Surgeon General (the only health app game to receive this honor). Embracing entrepreneurship takes a certain scrappiness and a willingness not to lose sight of your vision when everything feels against you or like you are Sisyphus pushing that fucking boulder up a hill.

Despite the struggle being real, on the plus side, entrepreneurship can be a way to control your work life and give you the opportunity to build something great. And to feel the swell of pride when that business succeeds since you will know that you built it yourself and realized your dreams.

So if you feel like a small voice in your heart or head is saying, "Hey, you, you should try this. You CAN DO IT!" like you're Adam Sandler in the film *The Waterboy* you may want to consider launching your own thing and seeing where it takes you.

As Lao Tzu said, "The journey of a thousand miles begins with one step." And that applies to self-employment, working as an employee, being a student, being in a romantic relationship, or even reading this book. One step starts every journey of our lives.

Thank you for reading this far. We are grateful to be on your journey with you. If you want to say hey, ask for advice, or let us know what you thought of our book, drop by https://mycompanyswipedleft.com or follow us on IG @helpmycompanyswipedleft

CHAPTER 9

You Can Do It!

GETTING LET GO FROM A JOB SUCKS. BUT it also gives you opportunities that you didn't know you might want.

When you're stuck in the corporate doldrums, you may be too comfortable with what you have or too worried about possible futures or failures so you shrink from other things you really want to do.

Now you have the chance to get a better workplace and a new boss, maybe go into a new industry, or have your own business.

The possibilities are endless. For example:
- A better company

- A boss who gets you

- A job that better suits your needs

- A job with better growth and development

- A chance to explore new industries

Is it easy? No, of course not. It's going to be rocky and uncomfortable, and some days you may think your life sucks. Other days you're going to go back into armadillo mode and just want to hide on your couch with bags of potato chips. And that's okay. Because there are going to be many days that you feel relieved and happy and excited.

The job that let Laura go unexpectedly by leaving her a voicemail message was one that she really didn't like. She realized there was a mismatch between what she wanted to do and where the company was going. She didn't like the culture, the product, or her boss. But she was too scared to leave. Sure it was a crummy job, but it was a job.

She had half-heartedly started to look for other positions, but she felt she didn't have to rush because she had the luxury of having a paycheck. When she lost that job, she felt it was like the universe saying, "WAKE THE FUCK UP!"

If she had not gotten that wake-up call she might have stayed there, growing more and more miserable while barely looking elsewhere. The job loss forced her to quickly pivot and spring into action. It was an incredibly stressful time. But looking back, it was a positive turning point in her career. It allowed her to take a contract job which gave her the time and energy to be able to focus on intentionally finding a role that was different from what she had been doing and more aligned with what she wanted to do and where she wanted to go with her career.

Your job loss can also be a positive turning point. You didn't have control over losing your job, but you have control over your actions now. You have a choice. You can feel shitty and stuck in your situation or you can acknowledge the pain and decide that you want to move forward.

It won't be smooth sailing and you may not get the job you want right away, but you can and will move forward. When Laura and Jill coach people how to tackle a major goal they say, "It may seem impossible at first. It's like thinking about hiking up a steep hill but it looks too hard. If you only focus on how high it looks from where you are, you might be too discouraged to get started. But if you decide to look down at your feet and focus on each step, that's doable. You can go step by step. Then when you look up again, you'll see how much you've advanced and realize that the top of the hill is not too far away."

Today, take one small step—not for mankind but for yourself. And then another. And another. Each step will get you closer to where you want to be: a new job that's a much better place for you.

YOU CAN DO IT!

Thank you

Acknowledgements and Gratitude

LAURA WANTS TO THANK her wonderful family and friends who encouraged and supported her during her job searches. She especially wants to recognize her marvelous Aunt Fran who always had positive things to say. She also appreciates her incredible and resilient daughter, Julianne, who is great at bouncing back.

Thank you to Lesa Edwards, a career coach with helpful information and insights. For more information about Lesa, Exclusive Career Coaching, her podcast, and the many resources that she offers, go to https://exclusivecareercoaching.com.

A big thank you to her dear friend, Barbara Limmer. Laura can always count on Barbara for amazing career advice.

And a GIANT thank you to her friend and co-author, Jill. Laura feels so fortunate to be able to partner with her.

JILL IS GRATEFUL FOR the readers of all of her books, and to her husband and dogs for granting her the time to write, to coach clients, and to handle household chores when deadlines are tight. And that she has the opportunity to co-create regularly with Laura.

She never realized the past thirty plus years of

employment and entrepreneurship would yield such rich materials and life lessons, but she's glad that it has and for the opportunity to share what she's learned with others so they don't need to repeat her mistakes. :)

    The best part of life is that we get to swipe right and left as much as we need and want to, but may you, dear reader, confidently swipe right on the best employment options for yourself. Godspeed.

The Authors

Jill L. Ferguson is an award-winning writer, the author of many books, and a business consultant. *LA Weekly* named her one of the top coaches to follow at the end of 2022. She thrives on collaborating with others and helping people reach their goals. She can be reached through her website at www.jillferguson.com.

Laura C. Browne is a corporate trainer, speaker, author, and business coach who works with individuals and companies to help them to be more successful. She has coached and trained leaders at Fortune 100 companies. She has written for *Forbes* and has been quoted as an expert in major publications including *USA Weekend*, *Cosmopolitan*, and *Family Circle Magazine*. She can be reached at www.careertipsforwomen.com.

Jill and Laura can also be reached at https://www.mycompanyswipedleft.com

www.ingramcontent.com/pod-product-compliance
Lightning Source LLC
Chambersburg PA
CBHW051955290426
44110CB00015B/2257